Schools

Around the World

Clare Lewis

Heinemann
LIBRARY
Chicago, Illinois

Edited by Joanna Issa, Shelly Lyons, Diyan Leake, and
Helen Cox Cannons
Designed by Cynthia Akiyoshi
Original illustrations © Capstone Global Library Ltd 2014
Picture research by Elizabeth Alexander and
Tracy Cummins
Production by Victoria Fitzgerald
Originated by Capstone Global Library Ltd
Printed in the United States of America in
North Mankato, Minnesota.

042015
008911RP

Library of Congress Cataloging-in-Publication Data

Lewis, Clare.
  Schools around the world / Clare Lewis.
     pages cm.—(Around the world)
  Includes bibliographical references and index.
  ISBN 978-1-4846-0370-3 (hb)—ISBN 978-1-4846-0377-
2 (pb) 1. Schools—Juvenile literature. I. Title.

LB1513.L49 2015
371—dc23   2013040504

Acknowledgments

We would like to thank the following for permission to
reproduce photographs: Alamy pp. 8 & 22d (© Steve
Morgan), 10 (© Jochen Tack), 11 & 23b (both © Bill
Bachman), 14 (© Robert Harding Picture Library Ltd);
Corbis pp. 9 & 22c (both © David Bathgate), 12 (©
Ocean), 21 (© Ian Lishman/Juice Images); Getty Images
pp. 5 (David Leahy), 6 & 22a (both UIG), 16 (NOAH
SEELAM/AFP), 17 (StockLite), 18 (Chris Schmidt), 19
(Shannon Fagan); Shutterstock pp. 1 (© Brenda Carson),
2 (© Kozini), 3 (© JasonCPhoto), 15 (© Hurst Photo), 20
& 22e (both © Dmitry Berkut); Superstock pp. 4 (Exotica
im / Exotica), 7 (Stock Connection), 13 & 22b (both
Biosphoto), 23a (Stock Connection).

Cover photograph of Buddhist monks in a classroom
in Sri Lanka reproduced with permission of Superstock
(Cusp). Back cover photograph reproduced with
permission of Shutterstock (© Hurst Photo).

Every effort has been made to contact copyright holders
of material reproduced in this book. Any omissions will
be rectified in subsequent printings if notice is given to
the publisher.

Contents

Schools Everywhere

Children go to school all over
the world.

Children go to school to learn.

Different Types of Schools

Some schools are in cities.

Some schools are in the country.

Some schools are outside.

This school is on a boat.

Some schools are at home.

Some children talk to their teachers on the Internet.

How Do Children Get to School?

Some children go to school on
a bicycle.

Some children walk to school.

Some children go to school on a boat.

Some children go to school on
a bus.

What Do Children Learn at School?

Children learn to read and write.
Children learn to do math.

Children learn about other countries.
Children learn about art and music.

What Else Do Children Do at School?

Children meet their friends at school.

Children eat at school.

Schools are different all over
the world.

What do you like to do at school?

Map of Schools Around the World

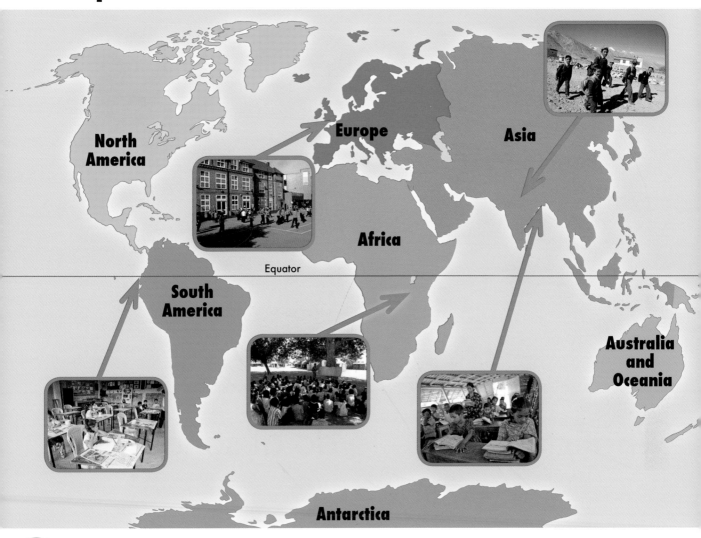

North America

Europe

Asia

Africa

Equator

South America

Australia and Oceania

Antarctica

Picture Glossary

country place that is away from towns and cities

Internet way of using computers that allows people who are far away to share information

Index

Notes for parents and teachers
Before reading

Ask children why they think they go to school. Ask them if they have ever been to any other schools before. What things were similar? What things were different? Show children a globe or map of the world and identify the continents. Explain that children go to school all over the world, and ask them to think about how schools in the book are similar and different as they read the book.

After reading

- Review pages 12–15 about how children get to school. Ask children how they got to school today and make a class graph to record and compare the different ways.

- Point out the map on page 22 and identify the continents with children. Demonstrate how to use the map to identify the continent on which different photos from the book were taken. Ask children where the photo on page 9 was taken (Asia). Have children look at the photo and discuss or list what things are similar and different between that school and their school.

Note on picture on page 12: NEVER ride a bicycle without a helmet.